GEOGRAPHY OF THE US
WESTERN STATES
(California, Arizona, Colorado And More)

GEOGRAPHY FOR KIDS - US STATES
5TH GRADE SOCIAL STUDIES

In this book, we're going to talk about the geography of the western section of the United States. So, let's get right to it!

The western section of the United States has vast deserts, tall mountains, and spectacular canyons. It is the largest region of the United States and it's also the most diverse.

YELLOWSTONE RIVER

MONTANA

The state of Montana has two completely different types of topography. The eastern and central regions of the state are an extension of the western part of the Great Plains. There are gently rolling hills with small clusters of mountains here and there. There are many river valleys formed by the two most important rivers in the state, the Missouri River and the Yellowstone River.

The western part of the state is a section of the Rocky Mountains. The Rockies are actually composed of several different mountainous ranges separated by different river valleys.

Some of the valleys have mountain lakes that were originally formed by glaciers. Mountain ranges in the northwest section of the state are the Bitterroot, the Swan, and the Lewis.

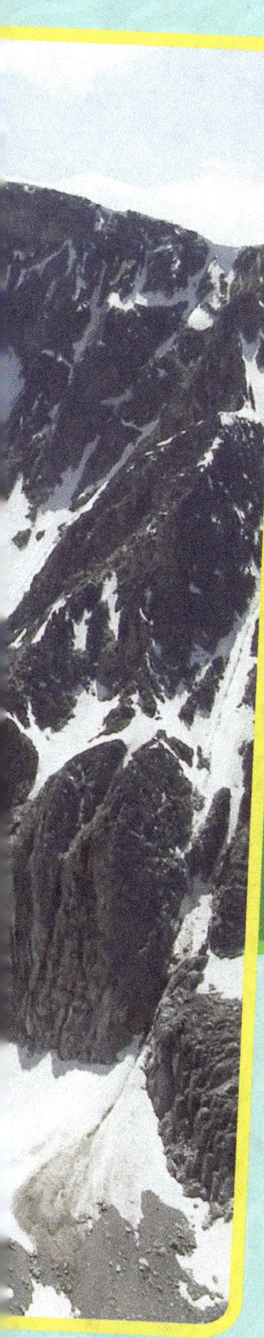

In the central and southern sections are the ranges of Little Belt, Big Belt, Crazy, and Pioneer. The state's highest elevation is Granite Peak with its height of 12,799 feet above sea level. It's located near the border with Wyoming to the south.

WYOMING

The Rocky Mountains dominate the state of Wyoming. There are at least 12 separate mountain ranges that run from the northwestern region to the southeastern region. They cover a large section of the state and form the Continental Divide.

GRAND TETON NATIONAL PARK, WYOMING

ABSAROKA MOUNTAIN RANGE IN WYOMING

The Continental Divide separates the waterways that travel into the Atlantic Ocean, Artic Ocean, and Gulf of Mexico from those that travel into the Pacific Ocean. Along the western border, there are the Wyoming, Teton, Gros Ventre, Snake River, and Absaroka ranges.

In the southeast, the Goshen range and the Laramie range rise up. In the center of the state, there is the Big Horn range in the north and in the south, there's the Medicine Bow Range. The average elevation of all the mountains in the region is 6,700 feet, which is second only to the state of Colorado. In the Wind River Range, Gannett Peak is the tallest mountain in the state at 13,804 feet.

Winding through the state between the mountains is the Intermontane Basins. These mountains are mostly flatlands that are dry and have low-lying grasses. They are mostly named by their surrounding mountains. In the southeastern edge of the state, the Great Plains extends into the borders of Wyoming and the land is ideal for cattle ranching. In the northeastern corner of the state are the Black Hills, most of which are in South Dakota.

COLORADO

The westernmost edge of the Great Plains is in the eastern section of Colorado. This region has the lowest elevation in the state. The terrain rises gradually until it gets to the base of the Rocky Mountains. The Rockies cover a major portion of the middle of the state with many towering peaks that surpass 14,000 feet in height.

The Continental Divide separates the eastern and western Rocky Mountain ranges. It also marks the location of the dividing line between the waterways that drain to the east and those that drain to the west.

The eastern Rockies in Colorado have the Front and Laramie ranges. In the south, the Sangre de Cristo Mountain range crosses the border into New Mexico.

A large area of flatlands, the San Luis Valley separates Sangre de Cristo from the southwestern mountain range of the San Juan Mountains.

Much of the western portion of the state is covered by the Colorado Plateau, which has many mesas, such as the White River Plateau. Mesas have flat tops and steep sides. The Rio Grande River starts in the south-central section of the state and flows south into the state of New Mexico. Grand Lake is the largest of the natural lakes.

NEW MEXICO

The Great Plains that cover most of the central region of the United States extend into the eastern part of New Mexico. The Rocky Mountain region extends from the state of Colorado into the north-central portion of New Mexico.

The Rio Grande River Valley separates the San Juan Mountains from the range of Sangre de Cristo. The highest mountain elevations in the state are found there. Wheeler Peak near the city of Taos is the highest peak at 13,161 feet.

CARLSBAD CAVERNS NATIONAL PARK, NEW MEXICO

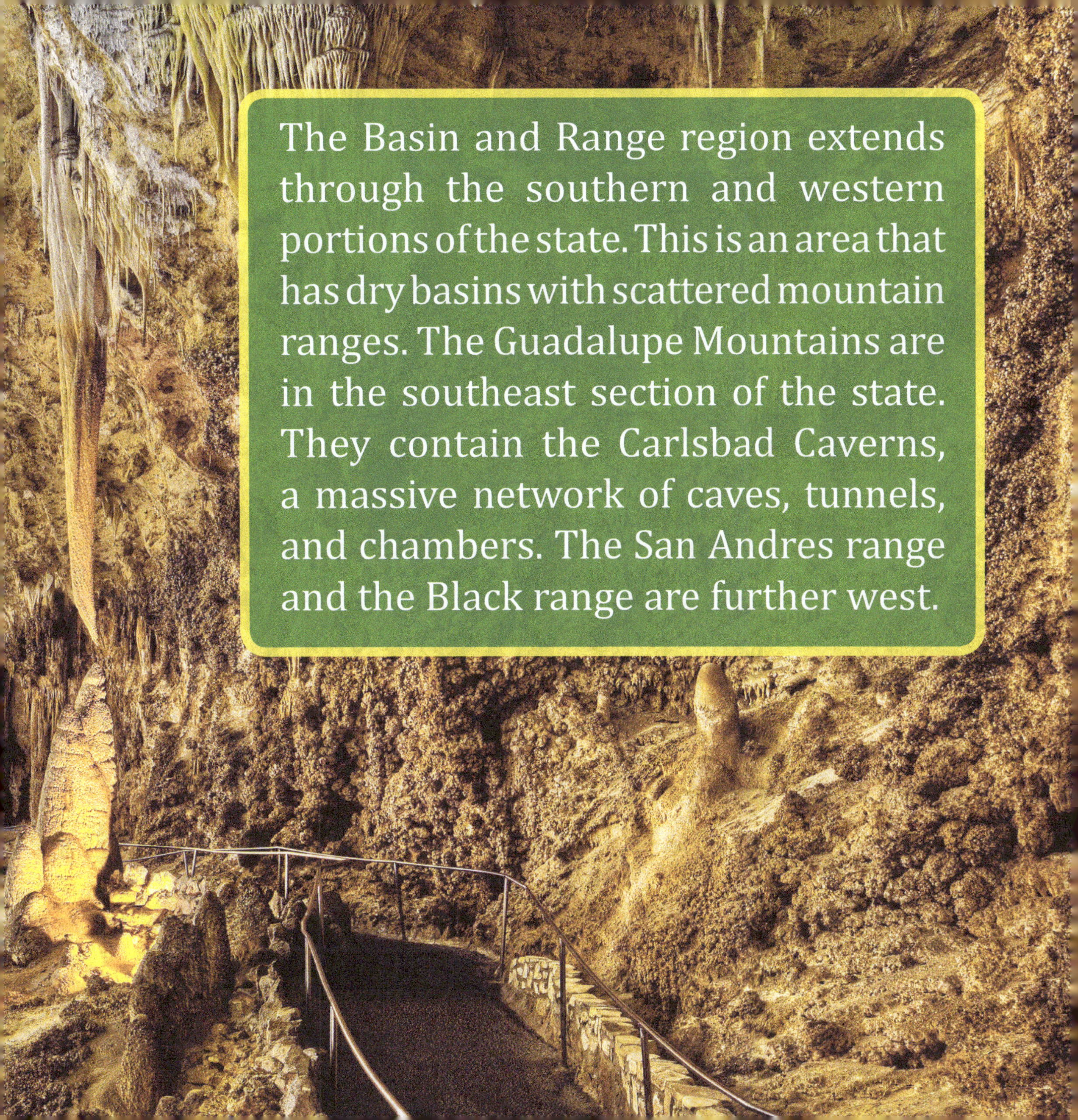

The Basin and Range region extends through the southern and western portions of the state. This is an area that has dry basins with scattered mountain ranges. The Guadalupe Mountains are in the southeast section of the state. They contain the Carlsbad Caverns, a massive network of caves, tunnels, and chambers. The San Andres range and the Black range are further west.

RIO GRANDE RIVER

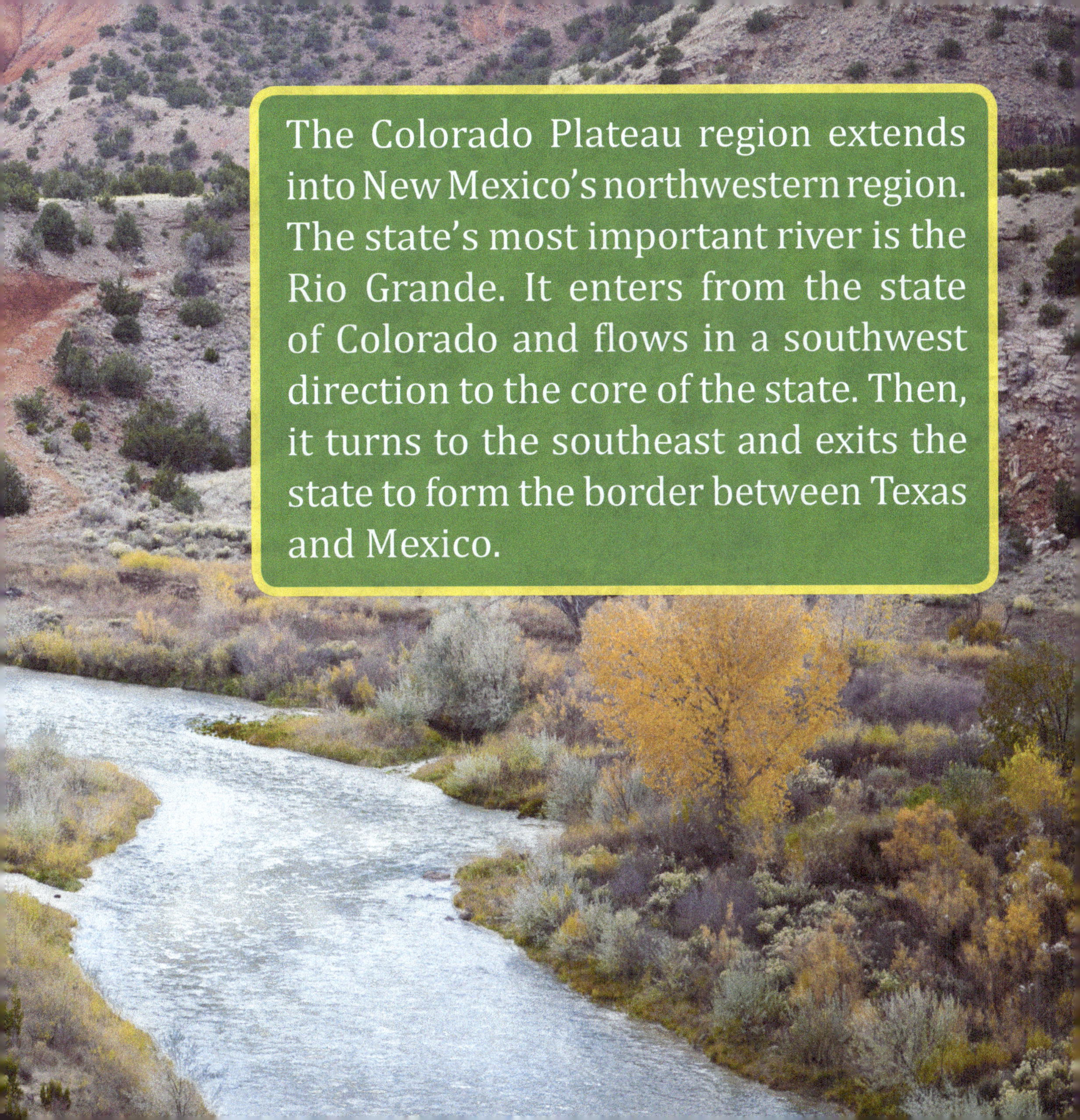

The Colorado Plateau region extends into New Mexico's northwestern region. The state's most important river is the Rio Grande. It enters from the state of Colorado and flows in a southwest direction to the core of the state. Then, it turns to the southeast and exits the state to form the border between Texas and Mexico.

IDAHO

Most of the state of Idaho is covered by mountainous regions. The Rockies extend over the northern, the eastern, and the central sections of the state. The terrain is rugged mountainous terrain with deep river valleys in between. The Bitteroot Mountains are on the border with Montana. In eastern Idaho, the Beaverhead Mountains and the Lost River Mountains are major landmarks.

BEAVERHEAD MOUNTAIN

MT. BORAH

The tallest peak in the state is in the Lost River Range at Borah Peak, which is a height of 12,662 feet. The southern part of the state is covered by the Snake River Plains of the Columbia Plateau.

The Snake River is one of the longest in the United States. It travels a distance of 1,020 miles.

UTAH

There are three distinct regions of terrain in Utah. The northern region and the northeastern regions of the state are covered by the Rockies. The highest elevations in Utah are found in the Uinta Range that extends west from the state of Colorado. Kings Peak, which has a height of 13,528 feet, is in the Uinta Range. The second distinct region is the area covered by the Colorado Plateau in the south and east regions of the state.

KING'S PEAK

It is characterized by different types of plateaus, such as buttes, which are isolated hills with steep sides, and mesas. These plateaus are cut by deep river valleys. The third distinct region is the Great Salt Lake Desert, which is the bed of an ancient lake, in the west of the state. The Great Salt Lake, located in this desert, is the largest natural US lake that's west of the Mississippi River.

ARIZONA

The Colorado Plateau covers about two-fifths of the northern section of Arizona. The Coconino, Kanab, and Kaibab Plateaus are in the northwestern section of this plateau region. The Colorado River cuts these plateaus in half carving the majestic Grand Canyon through them. The Grand Canyon is 1 mile deep and over 200 miles in length. The Painted Desert is in the north-central part of Arizona and is mountainous. East of the Painted Desert is the Petrified Forest, which contains an abundance of fossils.

PETRIFIED FOREST

In southern Arizona, the border between the Northern Plateau Region and the Basin and Range region is the Mogollon Rim, which extends for 200 miles. This area has several mountain ranges including the White Mountains and the Santa Maria Mountains.

Southwestern Arizona has the Sonora Desert with its distinctive red soil and other arid stretches of land between sparse mountainous areas.

NEVADA

Almost the entire state of Nevada is covered by the Basin and Range region of mountainous areas interrupted by dry basins. The mountains there are oriented in a north to south direction. In the eastern part of the state there are the Snake, Toana, and Ruby Mountains. In the central region, there are the Santa Rosa and Toiyabe ranges.

RUBY MOUNTAIN

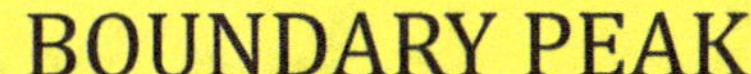

In the west of the state are the Wassuk, Humboldt, Stillwater, and Pine Forest ranges. The highest elevations statewide are in the southwest region with Boundary Peak rising 13,140 feet on the border with California. Lots of the bodies of water in the Basin areas, such as Carson Sink and Humboldt Salt Marsh, are filled with saltwater. The southwestern region of the state is crossed by the Sierra Nevada mountain range, which is primarily in California. Lake Tahoe, a popular resort, lies on the border with California.

WASHINGTON

The Coast Range region extends north from Oregon and covers the southwest corner of the state. Overlooking Willapa Bay are the Willapa Hills, a prominent feature in this part of the state. The Olympic Mountains are in the northwest section of the state with the Pacific Ocean to their west and the Strait of Juan de Fuca to their north. This part of Washington is wilderness and there are areas that have never been explored. Between the Coast Range and the Cascade Mountains is the Puget Sound lowlands including Puget Sound, which is a large saltwater bay. East of these lowlands is the Cascade Mountain range, which has mostly dormant volcanoes, except for Mount Saint Helens, which caused massive damage and loss of life when it erupted in 1980.

MOUNT ST. HELENS

MOUNT HOOD OREGON

OREGON

The Coast Range of mountains and the Cascade mountains are separated by the fertile Willamette lowlands fed by the Willamette River. Mount Hood, Oregon's highest mountain peak, which rises to 11,245 feet, is in the Cascade range. Where the Coast and Cascade ranges meet in the southwest corner of the state are the Klamath mountains. About 50% of the state is covered by the Columbia Plateau region. This vast area was formed by ancient volcanic activity that has been transformed into tall, forested mountains and spectacular canyons. Much of the southern part of the state is covered by the Basin and Range region.

CALIFORNIA

Much of the eastern part of California is dominated by the Sierra Nevada Mountain range, interrupted by the beautiful Yosemite Valley. The Sierra Nevadas contain several peaks over 14,000 feet including Mount Whitney, the highest peak in the continental US at 14,494 feet. West of the Sierra Nevadas is the Central Valley. This low, fertile agricultural area runs for more than 400 miles and is fed by the Sacramento and San Joaquin Rivers.

MOUNT WHITNEY

MOJAVE DESERT, CALIFORNIA

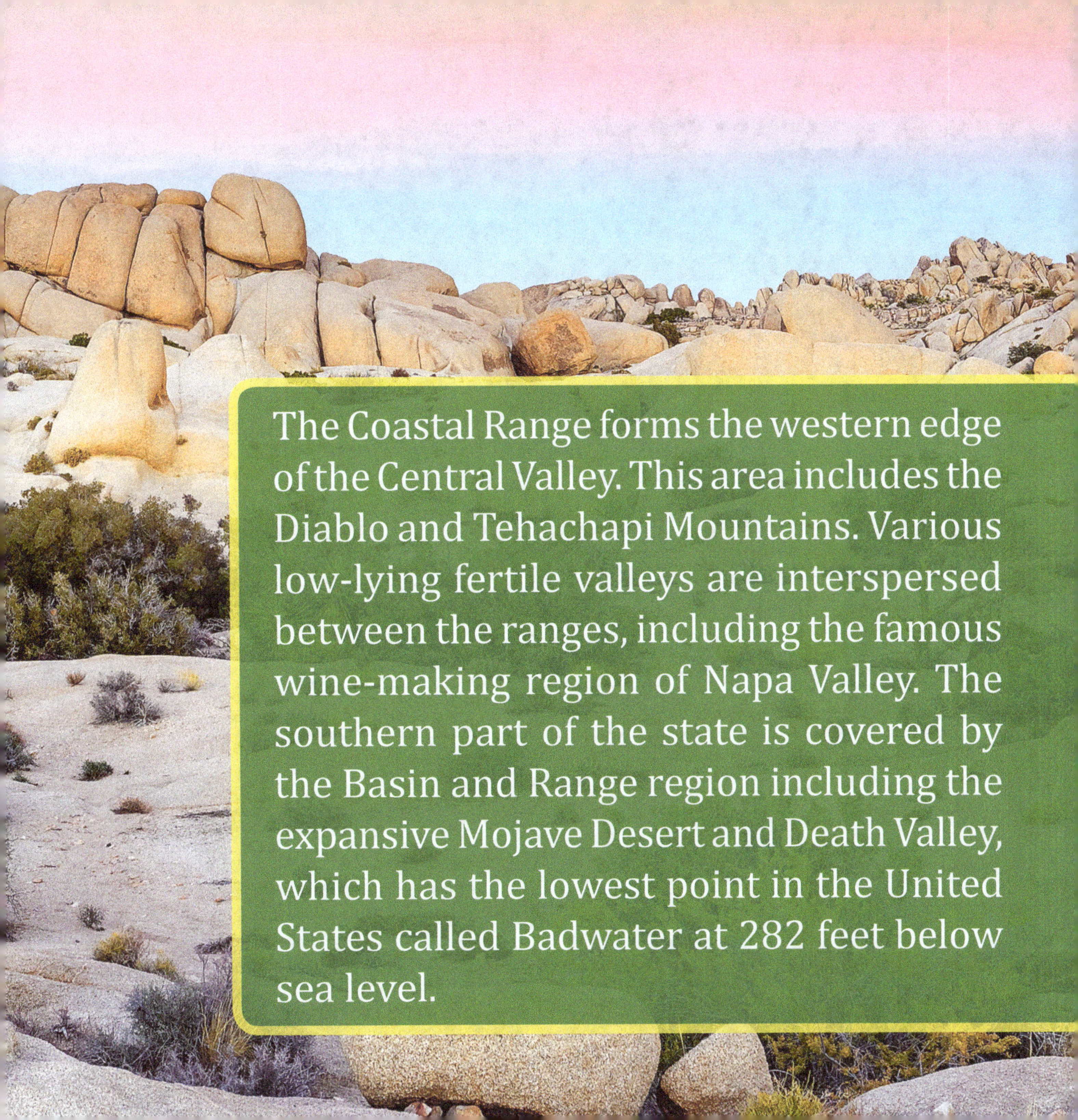

The Coastal Range forms the western edge of the Central Valley. This area includes the Diablo and Tehachapi Mountains. Various low-lying fertile valleys are interspersed between the ranges, including the famous wine-making region of Napa Valley. The southern part of the state is covered by the Basin and Range region including the expansive Mojave Desert and Death Valley, which has the lowest point in the United States called Badwater at 282 feet below sea level.

SUMMARY

The western states are known for their desert plateaus and plains, their forested mountains, including the Sierra Nevada and Rocky Mountain ranges, and their long strips of coastline facing the Pacific Ocean. The Grand Canyon in Arizona and Mount St. Helens in Washington are two of its many important geographic features.

Awesome! Now that you've read about the geography of the western section of the United States, you may want to read more about United States geography in the Baby Professor book The US Geography Book Grade 6: Deserts, Lakes, Rivers and Mountain Ranges.

Visit
BABY PROFESSOR
EDUCATION KIDS
www.BabyProfessorBooks.com
to download Free Baby Professor eBooks
and view our catalog of new and exciting
Children's Books